THE RIG VEDA

A HISTORY SHOWING HOW THE PHOENICIANS
HAD THEIR EARLIEST HOME IN INDIA

SALMON BOOKS

THE RIG VEDA

A HISTORY SHOWING HOW THE PHOENICIANS HAD THEIR EARLIEST HOME IN INDIA

Rajeswar Gupta

Late of the Bengal Provincial Educational Service

SALMON BOOKS

Chennai New Delhi

SALMON BOOKS

ISBN 9789349032149

Printed and bound in India
MJP 101
Salmon Books
No. 44, Nallathambi Street,
Triplicane, Chennai 600 005

Publisher: **C. Janarthanan**

PUBLISHER'S NOTE

The legacy of a country is in its varied cultural heritage, historical literature, developments in the field of economy and science. The top nations in the world are competing in the field of science, economy and literature. This vast legacy has to be conserved and documented so that it can be bestowed to the future generation. The knowledge of this legacy is slowly getting perished in the present generation due to lack of documentation.

Keeping this in mind, the concern with retrospective acquiring of rare books has been accented recently by the burgeoning reprint industry. Salmon Books is gratified to retrieve the rare collections with a view to bring back those books that were landmarks in their time.

In this effort, a series of rare books would be republished under the banner, "Salmon Books". The books in the reprint series have been carefully selected for their contemporary usefulness as well as their historical im-portance within the intellectual. We reconstruct the book with slight enhancements made for better presentation, without affecting the contents of the original edition.

Most of the works selected for republishing covers a huge range of subjects, from history to anthropology. We believe this reprint edition will be a service to the numerous researchers and practitioners active in this fascinating field. We allow readers to experience the wonder of peering into a scholarly work of the highest order and seminal significance.

Salmon Books

PREFACE.

Many truths lie buried in the dark depth of the past covered over by numerous strata of forgotten events. I propose to dig up one of them, one that would have to combat the history of the primitive ages as it is commonly accepted and also the cherished theories of the scholars of the east and the west, both old and new. What I fear is that the importance of the discovery may fail to attract the attention of the learned world through my own insignificance, utterly unknown to fame as I am. But I consider the task I have set upon myself to be of great moment, and nothing undaunted I intend to strike out the path, for diligence in the cause of truth is destined to bring its reward and recognition of the truth itself.

I begin by recapitulating first the results of my investigation to create, if possible, an interest in the subject at the outset. They are the following: —

I. A great war broke out in the remote old days between the Indian Aryans and the Phœnicians in which the latter were defeated and compelled to leave wholly or partially the land of the Aryans.

II. Most of the *Suktas* of the RIG VEDA either describe or refer to this and many other wars.

III. The RIG VEDA, therefore, is not a poem only but a history. The current meanings of most of the *Suktas* will accordingly have to be altered and the RIG VEDA SANHITA itself explained in a way different from the accepted one.

IV. The Phœnicians were the first of the civilized nations of the world. The civilization of Assyria, Babylonia, Egypt, Greece and other ancient countries owed its origin to the union of the civilization of the Aryans with that of *the Phœnicians.*

V. The Phœnicians originally lived in Afghanistan some part of India, whence driven out they migrated dually westwards. While still residing in the neighb hood of India they colonized and traded with Arabia the countries bordering on the Red Sea and the Medit nean Sea.

VI. The Phœnicians had colonies in many coun from each of which they were driven away by the na after severe struggles. In this way they were expelled India, Egypt, Greece, and Rome, or they mixed with natives when they lost their supremacy in those countries

VII. The primitive civilization of the world was l long before the time known to us.

VIII. In ancient time the Red Sea and the Medite nean Sea were connected together by a strait through w the Phœnician and Aryan trading ships entered the M terranean Sea and Indian goods were taken to Europe. that passage gradually silted up the connection betw India and Europe broke off.

These conclusions will lead on to many others whic is neither the place nor the time to dilate upon. They sure to revolutionize the history of the world, chalk a new path for linguistic researches, and recast the classifi tion of the human races when the agitation caused by th novelty has calmed down and they have found accepta with the learned world. A careful investigation, I am confid will reveal the truth of these statements to honest enquir and the feeble track I lay out will before long turn to a hi road in skilled hands of willing labourers in the cause.

——:-:——

THE RIG VEDA,

A HISTORY.

THE PANIS.

The word *Pani* occurs in not less than 36 *riks* of the RIG VEDA. It is used in one form or another in all the *Mandalas* except the fifth and the ninth, the forms being *Panih*, *Panim*, *Paneen* and *Panayah*. In the *Sukta* no. 108 alone of the tenth *mandala* the word is employed eight times. A list of the *riks* containing the word is given below :—

Mandala	*Sukta*	*Rik*
I	32	11
	33	3
	93	4
	124	10
	151	9
"	182	3
II	24	6
III	58	2
IV	25	7
	58	4
VI	20	4
	33	2
	39	2
	44	22
	45	31
	51	14
"	53	3, 5, 6, & 7
"	61	1
VII	6	3
"	9	2
	19	9

VIII	26	10
,,	75	7
,,	97	2
X	67	6
,,	108	–

There are 11 *riks* in the 108th *Sukta* of the *mandala,* and in six of them *Pani* is the god. In so the books the god is mentioned as *Panayah,* and in c as *Panayásura.*

It should be noted here that the names of the and the *Rishis* with which each *Sukta* begins were sel long after the collection of the VEDAS These were d mined in the Index known as the *Anukramanee.* *Anukramanee* which has been followed in the *Rik-Sa* in adopting the names of the gods and the *rishis*, was posed by *Katyayana.* *Katyayana* came after *Yáska*, anc therefore evident that the names were invented many turies afterwards without having any historic truth in tl There is nothing in the *Suktas* themselves which can tl any light in elucidating these words. Moreover in som the *riks* two or three names are mentioned of which only is to be taken as the god. It is clear the commen himself was at a loss to decide the point. It would have been the case had the composer of the *Sukta* mad selection himself. Had he done so he would surely mentioned only one god instead of many. Take for exa the 58th *Sukta* of the fourth *mandala.* The gods na therein are : —*Agni* (Fire), *Surya* (the Sun), *Ap* (Water), (the Cows), or *Ghrita* (clarified butter). The same rem apply to the use of the names of the *rishis, vide* the *Sukta* of the fifth *mandala* in which the names of the r are : – KUMÁRA, the son of ATRI, or KRISA, the son of or both. The inference therefore is that the names of *rishis*, the gods and the *chhandas* heralding each were inserted many years after the composition of *Sanhita itself,* and must accordingly be taken at the per worth. *Pani* and *Asura* are two different words with different meanings. The *Panis* were not *Asuras*. The application of the word *Panyásura* as the name of the god in the 108th *rik*, quoted above, is to be taken to date from the *Pauranic* period and not the *Vedic*.

THE STEALING OF COWS.

The stealing of cows by the *Panis* forms one of the most important factors of the *Rik-Sanhita*. The *Suktas* in which the *Panis* are mentioned, in which allusion is made to cows, or in which Indra is the god, are mostly related, directly or indirectly, to the stealing of cows. The commentator Sáyanáchárya admits this to be the case almost everywhere. Mr. Romesh Chunder Dutt, following the footsteps of Professor Max Muller, finds those of the *Suktas* or *riks* to contain the story of the stealing of cows in which the word *Pani* occurs, and considers the views of Sáyana as farfetched with regard to other *Suktas* and *riks*

In the commentary Sáyana makes reference to the *Panis* in explaining *Sukta* 33 of the first *mandala* (Vide page 79 of Mr. Dutt's edition), which runs : "Desiring to get back the cows, stolen by the Asuras known as the *Panis*, &c. Mr. Dutt rejects this allusion to the *Panis* on the ground that they are not mentioned in the *Sukta*. The list I have prepared will, however, show that the word *Pani* does occur in *rik* 3 of the *Sukta* and it may be noticed that Mr. Dutt has made no attempt to prove Sáyana wrong in his explanation there In my opinion Sáyana's exposition appears to be the correct one when we study the *Sukta* as a whole. Sáyana refers again to the story of the stealing of cows when he begins his commentary on Mandala II, Sukta 24, *rik* 6, and states how the homes of the Asuras of the *Pani* tribe were burned by the messengers of the *Devas* (gods) when they were discovered with the stolen cows by *the hound* Saramá. *Sukta* 108 of the tenth mandala will guide in opening up the secrets of those sacred books. must however at the outset say that my acknowledgme are due to the scholars who have already taken the lead unfolding the mysteries of the Vedas, as also to Mr. R. Dutt in particular.

The dispute is in regard to the correct meaning of three words, *Pani*, *Saramá* and *go*. For the meaning of first Prof: Max Muller depends on the meaning of the seco According to Prof. Kuhan, *Saramá* means storm. He sa that *Saramá* is only a different form of the Teutonic *Sto* and the Greek *herme*. The word *Saramá* is derived from root *Sar* with the suffix *amá*, and *Sar* means to go. *Sara* therefore means a runner or one who goes quickly. B storm or wind does not appear to be the correct meaning the word *Saramá* as used in the Vedas. There *Saran* is a messenger of Indra ; she seeks out the lost cows a goes about to distant places. For her services she is reward with food for her son, (I. 62. 3) and she gets a large quanti of milk from Indra and others (I. 72. 8). So *Saramá* cann mean the storm or the wind.

Prof. Max Muller would think that *Saramá* and tl early dawn were one and the same thing. He says : "The can be little doubt that she (Saramá) was meant for the earl dawn, and not for the storm. In the ancient hymns of th RIG VEDA she is never spoken of as a dog, nor can we fin there the slightest allusion to her canine nature. This is ev dently a later thought." Science of Language, Vol. II. P 51

I agree with the learned Professor in holding tha *Saramá* was not a dog. The *Panis* concealed the cows : *Sa amá* discovered them and informed Indra. It would appea that in those days whoever found out a lost thing afte a careful search—an informer—was called *Saramá*, an naturally the word came to mean a dog long after the Vedi days. To reconcile the meaning of the word in the Veda *Sáyana ascribes* to her supernatural powers, or how could dog *speak ? Nothing* was impossible in the land of the go

In the RIG VEDA *Saramá* has been given a number of attributes. She is the messenger of Indra (X. 108. 2); she is beautiful, fortunate (X. 108. 5); she is fair-footed or swift-footed. Surely these cannot be attributed to a dog.

Prof: Max Muller says: "It is Ushás, the Dawn, who wakes first (I. 123. 1); who comes first to the morning prayer (I. 123. 2). The sun follows behind as a man follows a woman (Rv I. 115. 2). Of whom is it said, as of Saramá, that she brings to light the precious things hidden in darkness? It is Ushás, the Dawn, who reveals the bright treasures that were covered by the gloom (I. 123. 6). She crosses the water unhurt (VI. 64. 4); she lays open the ends of heaven (I. 92 11); those very ends where, as the Panis said, the cows were to be found. She is said to break the strongholds and bring back the cows (VII. 75. 7; 79. 4). It is she who, like Saramá, distributes wealth among the sons of men (I. 92. 3; 123. 3). She possesses the cows (I. 123. 12. &c.); she is even called the mother of the cows (IV. 52. 2). The Angiras, we read, asked her for the cows (VI. 65. 5), and the doors of the dark stable are said to be opened by her (IV. 51. 2) In one place her splendour is said to be spreading as if she were driving forth cattle (I. 92. 12); in another the splendours of the Dawn are themselves called a drove of cows (IV. 51. 8; 52. 5). Again, as it was said of Saramá that she follows the right path, the path which all heavenly powers are ordained to follow, so it is particularly said of the Dawn that she walks in the right way (I. 124. 3; 113. 12). Nay even the Panis, to whom Saramá was sent to claim the cows, are mentioned together with Ushás, the Dawn She is asked to wake those who worship the gods, but not to wake the Panis (I. 124. 10). In another passage (IV 51. 3) it is said that the Panis ought to sleep in the midst of darkness, while the Dawn rises to bring treasures for man.

It is more than probable, therefore, that Saramá was but one of the many names of the Dawn"

Science of Language, Vol. II. pp. 512—513.

From these the Professor concludes that *Saramá* an *Ushá* or the dawn are the same thing. But I am unable t subscribe to this view. If *Saramá* could not be the storm, could neither be the dog. It is absurd that such epithets a fair-footed and beautiful should qualify a dog, or that suc expressions as *returning to Indra* and *crossing a strea* should be predicated of a storm.

The learned Professor was evidently so charmed wit the Greek stories of the light, the darkness and the daw that he was led to trace the allegory in the Vedas eve And it was very natural. The son of a famous Germa poet he was taught from his infancy to look upon the worl with the eyes of a poet as full of poetry. He loved poetr and saw it everywhere in nature all around. To him th RIG VEDA therefore was nothing but a poem, a book hymns, and hence the allegorical expositions. Thus wh was meant to be a history was taken to be a poem. Let m however point out that the RIG VEDA is not a poem but history, the first and the most ancient history of the worl It is impossible for a nation to have a poem without havin a history of its own. Prof: Max Muller would even trac the origin of the Trojan war in the epic of the immort HOMER to the stories of the *Panis* and *Saramá* in the RI VEDA.

To discover the original meaning of old and obsolet words it is necessary to know (1) the condition or histor of the then society, (2) the intellectual progress attained b the men of the time, and (3) the changes in the meanin which the words themselves have undergone from time t time. I would only point out here that at least the first tw requisites were not fulfilled by the Western scholars in asce taining the meaning of the Vedic words. In fact the alleg rical explanations they have given to various words passages of the RIG VEDA would point to an intellec state of our forefathers which it was not possible for t *to have* attained in those early days. Development of

Imagination must follow, and not precede the maturity of the Intellect.

The misconceptions of the Western scholars are more-over largely due to their acceptance of the current meanings of the Vedic words in explaining long-forgotten ideas and usages. It should be remembered that the modern meanings of words have reference to the modern state of the human society. An attempt to explain the Vedas, which are four or five thousand years old, in the light of present day signification of words is undoubtedly vain and useless. In two or three hundred years even many words and their meanings as well become obsolete and antiquated What wonder, therefore, that a large number of words of an ancient work like the Vedas should be entirely forgotten after the lapse of so many centuries? The use of many words in their original Vedic sense has been forbidden even after the days of Sáyana. The dictionaries which are the repositories of words and their meanings were themselves compiled long after the Vedas when a great many of the words had lost their etymological signification ; and the grammar has only puzzled the scholars in arriving at the correct import of the Vedic words, as it deals with but a few of the various meanings which particular words conveyed. Hence it is that the principal Vedic words have been made to mean what was not contemplated by the sages of old who used them first. The words *Saramá*, *Pani*, *Go*, *Indra*, *Soma*, the twins *Asvi*, etc., are of this class and difficult to unravel.

THE MEANING OF THE WORD

PANI.

I wish Prof. Max Muller had taken the same pains to ascertain the meaning of the word *Pani* as he had done for *Saramá*. To get at the correct meaning of the latter it is desirable that we should first know the correct meaning of the former And so I begin with the word *Pani*.

I have already said that the word *Pani* is mentione less than 36 times in the RIG VEDA The word *Pani* fo as it were the backbone of the RIG VEDA : it is the key t unfolds the meaning of the sacred book. Not only do stories of *Saramá* and *Pani*, but also a good many depend for their proper interpretation upon the cor meaning of the word *Pani* itself. The rules of gram relating to numbers and inflections have not been obser in the RIG VEDA and it is not unusual for a word in singular number to denote plural ideas or objects.

(1) The expression *Revatá Paniná* (4. 25. 7) shows t the *Panis* were rich.

(2) The expression *Paner maneeshám* (3. 58. 2) sho that the *Panis* were wise.

(3) *Abasam Panim* (6. 61. 1) would show that the *Pa* were given to introspection.

(4) The *rik* 7-6-3 tells us that the Panis did not perfo any *Yajnas* or sacrifices ; were garrulous, arrogant haughty ; had no respect for *Yajnas*, and were *Dasy* *i.e.*, idlers or robbers. According to *Sáyana* they w usurers also.

(5) In 1. 33. 3 the word *Pani* is used for traders. Dutt, evidently following the European scholars, adopts meaning of the term as *traders* in this *rik*. It is theref clear that the Panis were a trading people and sold thi for their value.

(6) The *rik* 6. 51 14 represents the *Panis* as gluttons. F their voracious eating they were regarded as monsters. T word is also explained to mean illiterate traders.

All these would go to show that the word *Pani* co never mean darkness. It must mean *men* or some cr tures akin to men. They were indeed a nation of trad without sacrifices, selfish, illiterate and usurious.

A nation of traders of those ancient days recal *Phœnicians* of old, for they were the only trading p then. *In those* days the Phœnicians were know

Panis. The Aryans spoke of them as the *Panih* and the Romans as the *Punic.*

The question now is, how did the *Panis* come to be the neighbours of the Aryans ?

Prof. Keightly says that the Phœnicians called themselves *Kedmus* In the Semitic language Keddum means the East. It is probable that the Phœnicians came from the east and so gloried in the name of Kedmus, i.e., an Eastern people This again would show that civilization had travelled from the east and had not its origin in Egypt.

Herodotus, known in the West as the father of History, was born in Asia Minor in 434 B. C. He travelled over many countries and recorded the experiences of his travels. He says: "The more learned of the Persians assert the Phœnicians to have been the original exciters of contention. This nation migrated from the borders of the Red Sea to the place of their present settlement, and soon distinguished themselves by their long and enterprising voyages. They exported to Argos, amongst other places, the produce of Egypt and Asia."—Chapter I. Book I.

Prof. Larchar of Ireland says: "Some authors make the Phœnicians to have originated from the Persian Gulf." And in Pockock's 'India in Greece' we have (vide page 218), "There to the north dwelt the singularly ingenious and enterprising people of Phœnicia Their first home was Afghanistan

I could multiply such quotations in support of my views. These lead me to conclude that from Afghanistan the Phœnicians went to the coast of the Persian Gulf, from the Persian Gulf to the borders of the Red Sea in Arabia and thence to Phœnicia, their last colony and home. I should like to observe here that they had, before their occupation of Phœnicia, colonized Egypt and the islands of the Mediterranean Sea. They had colonies in Greece and in the adjacent countries even. In fact with the Phœnicians or Panis *the light of* civilization travelled from the east to the west.

The Phœnicians held their own civilization to be most ancient and declared it to be thirty thousand ye old. There is however no doubt that they were one of first civilized nations of the world, if not the first, and t Phœnicia was not their first home. Instead of tracing th to their first settlements on the coasts of Arabia or Pe or in Afghanistan the historians of Europe have loca them at once in Phœnicia, and hence the mistake that po to the origin of all civilization in Egypt. I would not cuss here the question whether Afghanistan was the fi home of the Phœnicians or not. But I would affirm t the *Panis* or *Panih* of the RIG VEDA were the same peo as the ancient Phœnicians of Afghanistan.

——: :——

THE MEANING OF THE WORD GO.

After ascertaining the meaning of the word *Pani* I t up next the Vedic word *Go* *Saramá* will be the last w of my investigation.

The word *go* occurs in almost all the *riks* in which word *Pani* is used, and also in those *Sutras* in which In is the god or Ushá is the goddess. Prof. Max Muller generally explained *go* as the rays of the Sun.* I have yet been able to know how other Western scholars expl the word. Mr. Dutt has followed Prof. Max Muller has presented his view as shared by a number of Ve scholars. Sáyana interprets the word as *water* in cert passages, and as *the rays of the Sun* in others, *vide* 4. 5 and 4. 52. 2. There are, again, places where he gives no nonym for the word at all

Sáyana flourished in the fourteenth century A. D., w the Sanscrit vocabulary had been almost perfected. word *go* then had for its synonyms—Heaven, ray, thun *the moon,* the sun, animal, the cow-sacrifice, cow, w organ or sense, word, etc. And yet with all these before him Sáyana did not try to explain away the word *go* when he came across it in the incidents relating to the theft of the *go* by the *Panis*. A reference to the various passages will show that in such cases he has taken the word *go* to mean the *cow* or *cows* and not the rays of the sun.

Let us see how the RIG VEDA can itself help us in ascertaining the meaning of the word *go*.

It is said in 4.58.4 that the Panis kept concealed in the *go* three kinds of butter and the gods came to know of it. It is absurd to suppose that *go* which produced milk, curd and butter were rays of the sun and not cows. There cannot be the least doubt that *go* meant cows.

The conversation between the *Panis* and *Saramá* in the 108th *Sukta* of the tenth *mandala*, as translated into Bengali by Mr. Dutt, convincingly shows that the word *go* could not mean any thing but *cows*, that it meant some animal and not rays of the sun.

I quote below the passage as rendered in English by Professor Max Muller:—

(1) The Panis said: 'With what intention did Saramá reach this place! for the way is far, and leads tortuously away. What was your wish with us? How was the night? How did you cross the waters of the Rasá?'

(2) Saramá said: 'I come, sent as the messenger of Indra, desiring, O Panis, your great treasures; this preserved me from the fear of crossing and thus I crossed the waters of the Rasá.'

(3) The Panis: 'What kind of man is Indra, O Saramá? What is his look, he as whose messenger thou camest from afar? Let him come hither, and we will make friends with him, and then he may be the cowherd of our cows.'

(4) Saramá: 'I do not know that he is to be subdued, for it is he himself that subdues, he as whose messenger I came hither from afar. Deep streams do not overwhelm him; you, Panis, will lie prostrate, killed by Indra.'

(5) The Panis: 'These are the cows, O Saramá, which thou desirest, flying about the ends of the sky, O darling. Who would give them up to thee without fighting? for our weapons too are sharp.'

(6) Saramá : 'Though your words, O Panis, be unconquer though your wretched bodies be arrowproof, though the way to be hard to go, Brihaspati will not bless you for either.'

(7) The Panis : 'That store, O Saramá, is fastened to the r furnished with cows, horses, and treasures. Panis watch it wh good watchers ; thou art come in vain to this bright place.'

(8) Saramá : 'Let only the Rishis come here fired with S Ayasya (Indra) and the ninefold Angiras ; they will divide this s of cows ; then the Panis will vomit out this speech.'

(9) The Panis : 'Art thou, O Saramá, come hither driven b violence of the Gods ? Let us make thee our sister, do not go again ; we will give thee part of the cows, O darling.'

(10) Saramá : 'I know nothing of brotherhood or sisterhood ; dra knows it and the awful Angiras. They seemed to me anxiou their cows when I came ; therefore get away from here, O Panis, away.'

(11) 'Go far away, Panis, far away ; let the cows come out strai the cows which Brihaspati found hid away, Soma, the stones, and wise Rishis.'

THE MEANING OF THE WORD

SARAMA´.

If *Pani* means the Phœnician merchant and *go* the c it can easily be understood that Saramá cannot mean eit the (she) Dog of the gods or the Dawn. Professors M Muller, Monier Williams and others have taken the Ve story of the theft of cows as an allegorical representat of the conflict between light and darkness or day and nig Hence they have explained a good many *riks* as hymns praise of Nature I am sure these scholars have not every step followed the proper meaning of the Vedic wo but have adopted what they themselves thought to be th plausible meaning.

Saramá introduces herself to the *Panis* as the mess ger of Indra. I can safely affirm without stopping to *quire who Indra* was, that Saramá is neither a dog, nor *Dawn, but she is* human and she is a woman. It may interest to note that the Panis do not ask her who *she* is, but who *Indra* is, by whom she is sent to them. It is evident she is already known to them. The very conversation between them shows that they are not strangers. This leads me to infer that by Saramá is meant those Pani-women who with their children had been imprisoned by the Angiras. The Angiras and their party had compelled these *Saramás* or messengers to capitulate for them with the Panis. They could not leave their children without making due provisions for them (1-62-3) as they were afraid of being detained by the Panis. Or it may be that the Angiras forced the mothers to go out to the Panis as their messengers and kept the children as hostages for the successful performance of their duty.

It would seem that for some reason or other the study of the RIG VEDA was for many centuries forbidden, and so the present confusion about the meaning of the Vedic words. The age of the Puranas evidently had its origin in an attempt to discover the original meaning of those words. In their ignorance of the proper signification of the epithets the commentators thought out gods and goddesses hoping to give a rational explanation of the sacred books. Thus they were led to ascribe to inanimate objects desires and functions which they could never exercise or possess, forgetting that the words in question in the Vedas related to *men* and *their* actions. And thus did the age of the Puranas or Mythology come into existence clothing the Vedas with absurdities. Still however in the hands of the Indian scholars like Sáyana and others the Vedas were not wholly divested of their historical garb. But the Western scholars, on the other hand, led by Professor Max Muller, have gone a step further—they have declared the Vedas to be nothing more than hymns in praise of Nature. Hence the difference in the interpretations of the RIG VEDA by the savants of the East and the West. Investing the Vedas with mythical ideas Sáyana has interpreted Saramá to be the Dog-messenger of the gods, while to Max Muller and his followers she is only the storm or tl Dawn to suit their theory that the Vedas are but a collecti of hymns. In the latter is lost the vestige of historic wor of the Vedas that is still traceable in the former. I am l to discard both these views I accept the Vedas as a histo recording the actions of men—that this view is correct w be amply demonstrated in this treatise.

Sukta 108, quoted above, if properly interpreted, w show that Saramá could have been nothing but a woma In fact the expressions used therein cannot be correctly a rationally explained except in relation to man. For tl and various other reasons I have interpreted Saramá as imprisoned (or prisoner) *Pani* (Phœnician) woman.

Another point worthy of notice in this connection that all primitive words originally meant objects or thin Abstract or metaphorical meanings, as they implied intelle tual development, came in long afterwards. The RIG VE was composed in the primitive age of words and it w almost impossible for them to have been used metapho cally at that stage. The metaphorical and allegorical int pretation of the Vedas by the Western scholars cannot the fore be considered sound and reasonable.

———:-:———

THE CAUSE OF THE WAR.

I may now say with Sáyana that the *Panis* stole tl cows of the *Angirás* or of their friends. The *Angirás* d feated the *Panis* with the help of Indra and other power allies and regained their cows. I must however admit he that I am not yet certain whether the Panis stole the co of the Angiras or the Angiras attempted to take by force tl cows belonging to the Panis, for the Angiras and their par sans would not unoften seize the cows of others : vide Sukt 6-45-24 and 6-45-32. This shows that the Angiras wo *ask for cows* from *Kavitsa* and *Bribu*. Some of the own *would part with* their cows without any objection to co their friendship with the Angiras, but some would object and a fearful strife would ensue. The Angiras would ask the Panis to give them their cows, but they would not do so willingly. So the Angiras sometimes took their cows by force—vide 1-93-4. Many of the Aryan families were afraid of the Angiras and they would not oppose them. But the Panis were rich and powerful and possessed many hill forts and fortified towns : 6-45-9. So they were not afraid to defy the Angiras.

In *riks* 4-93-1 and 1-39-6 the cow is mentioned as an article of food. It is therefore evident that the Angiras were in the habit of taking beef and other meat. I have shown before elsewhere in my Bengali Journal the *Anjali*, Part 12, Vol. I) that the Indian Aryans used to take animal food and intoxicating drinks, for which they fought amongst themselves I am not yet sure if the Panis were Aryans, but there is no doubt that they had a terrific quarrel with the flesh-eating Angiras and their party for their cows and other cattle.

It is now necessary to determine who the Angiras were. They were the principal branch of the Aryans. *Rik* 2-24-6 describes them as learned. *Brahmanspati* or *Brihaspati* was their leader or headman. In *rik* 5-101-1 Sáyana interprets *Brahmané* in relation to the caste or the family of the Brahmans or the Angiras. This would show that the *Brahmans* of the later days were no other than the Angiras of the Vedic period. The word *Brahmavih* occurs in *rik* 9-33-1. Sáyana explains it as *Mantraih* that is *by incantations* or *the sacred words.* According to Pandit Ramanath Sarasvati the word means *by the worshippers.* Mr. Dutt however following Professor Wilson (and perhaps accepting the reading *Nibrahmavih*) makes it mean *by those who were unable to accept the mantras*, but says in the note that the meaning of the passage is not clear. I think the meaning would be clear enough if the word were taken to denote the Angiras. It should be remembered that according to *Sáyana* the Brahmans are the descendants of the Angiras.

The Angiras were flesh-eaters whilst the Panis were cowherds. That the flesh-eaters would often oppress the herdsmen can easily be understood. The Panis prepared three kinds of articles of food from the milk of their cows. Sáyana has described them as *Ksheer* or condensed milk, *Dadhi* or curd and *Ghrita* or clarified butter. I think the Persian *Panir* (cheese) is one of these three preparations. Most probably it is a modification of the first (condensed milk). The article was first prepared by the *Panis* and so the name *Panir* The Panis not only made these preparations but also traded in them, and hence their love and care of cows and other cattle. Their rivals the Angiras, however, would kill the animals for the sake of their meat. Their interests were thus diametrically opposed and they fought for the cows. I hold the Angiras to have been the aggressors.

I should mention here that to make the various preparations of milk the Panis required earthen pots and therefore knew the art of pottery and other kindred arts for making the requisite tools, etc. They also knew the art of cooking. The god "*Chatuh Sringah*" that is, having four horns, was nothing but a rod for churning milk and was used for preparing clarified butter. Another instrument was named the *Dasa Yantra Utsa* (6-44-24). It must have been a sort of lactometer. Different Vedic scholars have explained it differently though. There is however no doubt that the Panis knew how to cook and used to take cooked food. But the Angiras simply roasted their meat and other articles of food before taking them. This operation of roasting was known by such names as *Kratu* and *Yajna, i.e.*, sacrifice. It may be that particular terms were applied as the occasions were ordinary or special. The Angiras hated the Panis and called them *Akratu* and *Ayajna* (that is men who did not perform the sacrifice), as the latter were not in the habit *of roasting their* articles of food. On the other hand it can *easily be imagined* that the Panis treated the Angiras with contempt for their sacrificial observances. Such epithets as vain, arrogant, etc., applied to the Panis would show that the feeling of hatred originated with them. The hatred of the Angiras was merely reciprocal. The fact that the Panis were more advanced would only confirm my theory.

THE RIVALS.

In ancient times it was impossible for men to live in villages as at present. If they were afraid of the depredations of wild beasts, they were no less afraid of the outrages of human enemies which were yet more violent. For this the custom then was to live in *Gosthis* that is clans or communities. The Panis formed one such clan and they were further subdivided into houses or families. Each clan or house in those days lived in what is now called a *Busti* in the Upper Provinces of India. The *bustis* or localities were known as *nagars* or towns. The towns were protected by walls or trenches around them. I have already said that the Panis had many towns and forts and also an army. The clans of the *Asuras*, the *Ilibis*, the *Ahis*, the *Bals*, etc., were friends of the *Panis* and were opposed to the *Angirás*, the *Agnis*, the *Bayûs*, the *Marûts*, etc. The war they were engaged in might fitly be called the first *Kurukshetra* war. I believe all the rising families of ancient India took part in this great fight siding with one or the other party, and I have no doubt that branches of the *Dása* or the primitive families also had their share in it.

I take *Agni*, *Bayû*, *Marût* and others to represent different families or clans like the *Panis*. This I could prove not only from the RIG VEDA but from various other ancient works also. It is easy to see that the terms as used in the *Suktas* of the Vedas refer to *men*. Their present interpretation to denote natural phenomena or the elements in the various passages in which they occur in the Vedas, is more *modern*; the words originally meant families of men, but underwent a change in the course of time to acquire tł present meaning. Professors Max Muller, Kuhan and oth have tried to fix their meaning tracing them to their ro It should be remembered that the Vedic words had alrea lost their original import when their roots were formulat and an attempt to explain them in the light subsequen obtained could not meet with unqualified success.

The Panis and their party have in many places be mentioned as *Adevas* (*a*=no or not, and *devas*=gods). is therefore not strange if their enemies, the Angiras a their friends have been called *Devas*. The word *Arya* is comparatively modern origin though it, like the word *Dá* occurs in several *Suktas*, and so I cannot agree with thc who hold the Vedic war to have been a war between *Arya* and *non-Aryans*. The word *Arya* came to be applied to the clans including the *Panis*, the *Asuras*, the *Bals*, t *Angiras* and others, at a later period.

The frequent application in the RIG VEDA of the wor *pûrva* (old) and *nûtana* (new) is worthy of notice, as also t mention of Indra as *Yuvá*—a word used to qualify oth gods also. According to Mr. Dutt *yuvá* in several plac means *young*. But I think it means *new* to distinguish tl Indra of later days from the Indra of old. The constant u of these three words—*purva*, *nûtana* and *yuvá* lead me infer that the RIG VEDA contains a description not of o but of two great wars—one the Panik or Phœnician and tl other the *Asúrik* or pertaining to the *Asúras*. The Phœnicia war was the earlier of the two and it was in the days whe the old *rishis* or sages flourished: the Asurik war came aft when new *rishis* appeared. The Indra who figured in th *Panik* war had not the distinctive term *yuvá* which chara terised the Indra of the Asurik war. There may be *Sukt* relating to other wars, but these two were the most terrib and lasted long.

The Panis were not, however, the only trading peop *in those old* Vedic days. Many other nations and ra either singly or jointly with the Panis traded in various parts of the then known world. Perhaps all or most of them sided with the Panis while some families of the Panis themselves espoused the cause of the Angiras, vide *riks* 31, 32 and 33 of *Sukta* 45, *mandala* 6, regarding the *Bribus*. These Bribus, I think, were no other than the modern Brahui or Brahoe of Beluchistan for which reference may be made to Chamber's Encyclopædia, Vol II, or Encyclopædia Britannica, Vol. III. They were skilled carpenters. The *Tvastás* were a branch of these *Bribus*. Professor Max Muller has given an account of the *Bribus* in Vol. II of his "Chips from a German Workshop." According to him they were a family of carpenters from whom the *Rhibhús* also learnt the art. I think the *Rhibhús* who were allies of the *Angiras* learnt the art of carpentry from the *Bribus* who sided with the *Panis*. The fact is that all of them were *men* and not gods: vide *Suktas* 20 and 40 of the first *mandala*.

The word *Púshá* is mentioned in *Sukta* 42 of the first Mandala and also in several other Suktas. The Angiras were not acquainted with the whereabouts of the Panis and so sought the help of the Pushas in finding them out. The Pushas were thus the guide of the Angiras.

If we eliminate the more modern and the special Suktas we shall find that the RIG VEDA is a history of the Panik and the Asurik wars. The gods mentioned in them were friends of one or other of the parties engaged in the wars. They were all different branches of the ancient human race and not gods of the elements, nor deified powers of Nature.

——:o:——

MUTUAL HOSTILITY.

I have already said that the Angiras were hated by the Panis for their sacrificial rites. In fact the hatred was carried so far that the Panis appeared wherever the Angiras performed their sacrifices and caused great disturbances The Angiras retaliated by seizing and destroying the commodities as butter and cheese, of the Panis. The practice offering up *ghee* or clarified butter to the sacred fire may traced to the attempt of the Angiras to burn the *ghee* the obtained by plunder from the Panis. In this act the Angir had the support of their friends *Mitra* and *Varuna*: vic 1-2-7 in which they invoked the latter to their help.

Mercilessness in the treatment of the fallen enemy chara terised the spirit of vengeance in those remote old days. cannot say that the humanitarian civilisation of the prese day is without any trace of it. The captives were then ke in dark dungeons strongly bound in chains or cords, in th custody of the *Varunas* who acted as gaolers and were know as *Pasees* or Binders. It was the duty of the latter to secu the enemies in the field of battle when conquered and pu them in chains. Sometimes they would go out as pirat and surprise their enemies whom they would bring away i chains or cords. In the Suktas 24 and 25 of the fir *mandala* the *rishi* is mentioned as *Súnah Sep* which would appear to have been used as a general term for the Phœnicia prisoners These Suktas describe how they were secure by means of *pás*, that is, chain or cord. The following pa sages will help to make me clear :—

"Of the gods of various orders, whose graceful nam shall I utter? Who will again set me free in this wide worl that I may see my parents?" 1-24-

"May he (Varuna) chastise the enemy who has pierce my heart." 1-24-2

"I pray to you for long life" 1-24-1

"May the king set us at liberty." 1-24-1

"Unfasten from above, O Varuna, the upper cords tha bind us down and the lower ones from below. Loosen als the ties in the middle. We shall then, O thou son of Adit live sinless without breaking thy vows." 1-24-2

The above extracts show that those who were th *lamenting and* asking for mercy did not know the gods, we *They only* besought him for clemency who they thou could release them. It is therefore clear that these lamentations arose from the parties of the *Adevas* (no-gods) who were subjected to the cruellest torture when imprisoned by their enemies.

The enemies and their houses were burnt down in retaliation :—

"They (the Angiras) made fire with their own hands and hurled it on to the hills (the hill forts of the Panis), for the destroying fire was not there before."—2-24-7.

Thou hast burnt to ashes the robber captured from the land of the *Devas*. —1-33-7.

Jealousy and envy brought about a difference in the customs and usages of the opposing parties. I would trace the different modes of writing from right to left and from left to right to the mutual enmity of the *Devas* and the *Adevas* —the latter writing from right to left and the former from left to right. The Panis as traders had learnt early the art of writing for which the Devas disliked them. Even the Vedas remained unwritten for many centuries and continued as *Srutis* being committed to memory and thus handed down from generation to generation. From an aversion to writing, anything written was scorned or ridiculed as after the fashion of the Panis or Panisads. ***Panisad*** would appear to be the Greek name for Pani. Hence the name "U-Panisad" or "*Upanisad*" derived from a dislike to writing. In very many *riks* the term "U" or "Uh" has an interjectional use and is expressive of an emotion of pain or scorn. I think the word Upanisad (*Upanishad*) is born of scorn for the Panis. It is remarkable that the derivation of this word *Upanishad* is not yet satisfactorily traced A reference to the authorities extant will bear me out.

THE DATE OF THE PANIK WAR.

On the date of the Great Phœnician War depends the *primitive* history of man, for the age of the ancient civilisation of the world must count from that date. It would a present appear that history has not recorded any eve earlier than this war, and as our early civilisation is mainl related to the Panis and their times, the date of this wa must be a very important factor in our researches.

I hold with the Panis that they were the first of th civilised nations of the earth. If they were the first to se the light of civilisation, they did also, under the guidanc of Providence, spread that light among various peoples i the ancient world; in fact they carried it from one countr into another either to be expelled in the end or to merg themselves in the nationality of the people with whom the came in contact.

The Panis had colonies in Afghanistan, Persia, Arabia Turkey, Egypt and Greece, and their supremacy gaine ground in one when it declined in another. It will b enough for me to say for the present that facts are on recor which conclusively prove that the Panis at least visited a these countries for purposes of trade and they introduce India to other ancient countries of the world in those days.

Many are the adherents of the theory propounded b the Western scholars that from Central Asia the Aryan migrated to India and the other countries. It is not easy t determine exactly who these Aryans were. I am incline to think that originally there was no nation bearing tha name. The word as used in some of the *riks* of the Ri Veda does not appear to refer to any particular nation. Th word "Aryan" came to be used after the Phœnician Wa It is probable that the Angiras and their allies were give that name for their agricultural pursuits. This would nulli fy the theory of their migration from Central Asia. Afte the Great War the survivors of the rival parties who wer left together formed into a new nation under the name o the Aryans. The word *Asura* has been repeatedly used i *the Rig Veda*, and I have already shown elsewhere th *Assyria was named* after them to denote the country th lived in. After the war a branch of the great *Asura* clan passed over into Asia Minor and founded Assyria. In India they as well as their country had been known by the name of *Asura* This leads me to conclude that it was from India and not from Central Asia that the Aryans migrated into different lands using the trading ships of the Panis in their travels—a conclusion which dispenses with the theory of their migration overland also.

The Phœnician ships sailed from the coasts of India and entered direct the Mediterranean Sea through the *Strait* of Suez, for in those remote days Suez was a *strait* and not an *isthmus* as it afterwards became through the silting up of the channel. The subsequent closure of the passage not only broke off the communication between the East and the West but also separated the Panis inhabiting the two quarters. Hence it was that long afterwards India appeared as a dream land to the ancient Greeks and other nations. The Panik War had taken place long before the strait of Suez was closed. That Suez was originally a strait will be evidenced by the facts here adduced. The present isthmus is sandy, which shows that there was a time when it formed part of the sea. Geology will bear testimony to this. The following extracts also support my view :

"From hence inland to Heliopolis the country of Egypt is a spacious plain, which, though without water, and on a declivity, is a rich and sandy soil."

Herodotus. Book II, Chap. VII.

Again :—

"The greater part of the country (Egypt) described above, as I was informed by the priests, (and my own observation induced me to be of the same opinion) has been a gradual acquisition to the inhabitants. The country above Memphis, between the hills before mentioned, seems formerly to have been an arm of the sea."

Ibid. Book II, Chap X.

Helipopolis forms the basis of the great delta of the Nile in Egypt. To the east and the west of Heliopolis the soil is soft and clayey which conclusively proves that it has been formed by the alluvia of the Nile and that the cities of Heliopolis and Memphis stood in the olden days on the shores of the sea. It is therefore patent that the entire land to the east and the west in a line from Heliopolis to Memphis was under the sea, the Mediterranean and the Red Seas being connected together by the Strait of Suez. In support of this I quote Prof. Pococke who says, "The soil of Egypt, except what it has received from the overflowing of the Nile, is naturally sandy, it is full of nitre and salt."

I am further confirmed in my statement by Prof. Larcher, for he says :—

"If it be true, all the country from Memphis to the sea must have been formerly a gulf of the Mediteranean parallel to the Arabian gulf, the land must have been raised up little and little from a deposit of the mud which the waters of the Nile carry away with them."

All this would show that there was a time when Suez was under water through which the Phœnician vessels sailed to the Mediterranean, and Heliopolis was an important port of the Panis. It was when Suez was a branch of the sea with Heliopolis on it, or before that age even, that the great Phœnician war broke out. The union between the east and the west broke off as Suez turned into an isthmus.

The Strait of Suez had nearly silted up when Moses crossed the Red Sea and the Israelites—the last of the Panis—safely passed over the shallow water. According to many Moses flourished two thousand years before Christ, and it must have taken two thousand years more for Suez to have filled up. The fact that Heliopolis had then fallen into decay before the growing fame of Memphis, would support this theory. It is said that Menes, the first king of Memphis, founded the city more than four thousand years before Christ, and according to the Greeks the god *of the name* of Helios reigned in Egypt long before the date extending over a period of about fourteen thousand years. There can be no doubt that these rulers of Heliopolis, the so called gods Helios, were none other than the Panis of old. Heliopolis therefore must have fallen into ruins at least four thousand, if not six thousand years before Christ.

It should be noted here that Heliopolis was the cradle of the Egyptian civilisation of which the Panis were undoubtedly the originators.

According to the Western scholars the Rig Veda was composed in 2000 B. C. As I have already shown the Phœnician war to have taken place in 4000 B.C., the Rig Veda may safely be assumed to have been composed about that time. It should be remembered that the great Book took many years to compile and it is not improbable that a number of the *Suktas* were composed in 4000 B. C. I would even say that the *Pauranic* or Poetic Age began two thousand years before Christ. It is not therefore unlikely that the historical part of the Rig Veda was anterior to the *Pauranic* age by another two thousand years. Mr. Tilak, the well known Mahratta scholar, has, in explaining the astronomical import of a particular *Sukta*, demonstrated that the Rig Veda was composed six or seven thousand years before Christ. The Phœnician war, as recorded in the Rig Veda, may therefore be referred to a date at least six or seven thousand years before the Christian era, if not earlier.

CONCLUSION.

With a few words more I shall conclude the subject. In every nation or race, old or new, civilised or uncivilised, war-songs have been handed down from generation to generation. The small stock of songs that the wild hill tribes possess is only a collection of war-songs Colonel Todd's history of Rajasthan is based on such songs. In fact the songs of, *Bhâts* or eulogists, so well known in this country, were current even in the Vedic age, and I have no hesitatio in affirming that in war-songs and songs of victory the Ri Veda had its origin, at least they form the bulk of the grea work. The old war songs of ancient India composed th true Rig Veda and many other songs on various subject came to be added to them subsequently. The Rig Veda i thus not a collection of hymns and anthems but of wa songs recording the primitive history of the world. It may therefore be concluded that the first history of each natio or race of man began with war songs.

I have in the previous section already mentioned th city of Heliopolis of Egypt. In Greek "Heliopolis" mean "the city of the sun." In India also there was an ancient cit of that name which would appear to have belonged to som family of the Panis A city or town in those days would be named after the family or clan that inhabited it, and so the clan of the Heliopolis named their towns after their own wherever they went. This I conclude from the name *Ilibi* which occurs in the Rig Veda, the word being only anothe form of Heliopolis. All the towns of the name of Heliopoli —in India, in Egypt, or elsewhere—were founded by th *Ilibis*.

Modern Morea in Greece had for its ancient name Pelo ponnesus which I think originally meant *palli* or residenc of the Panis. That Greece was not unknown to the peopl of ancient India has been very ably shown by Prof: Po cocke in his work "India in Greece." In fact the fame c India was carried throughout the ancient world by suc races as the Ilibis, the Panis, the Bals, the Asuras an others.

If may be safely affirmed that Balkh, Baalbek and othe ancient cities bearing similar names were founded by th Bals. We know from the Rig Veda itself that the nort west of ancient India was inhabited by these races wh used to fight amongst themselves. The Rig Veda is th fore not only a history of ancient India but of the e ancient world, and so the whole human race is interested in its correct and proper exposition. And as more light is thrown on the subject new truths will be discovered in the various branches of human knowledge. For this purpose it is necessary that the great work should be translated in the different languages of the world.

When in the old days the isthmus of Suez was a strait connecting the Red Sea with the Mediterranean not only was there an exchange of merchandise between the countries on either side but also of thoughts and experiences. With the closing up of the passage such exchange ceased and the nations and races grew up independently each in its own way, the western nations making rapid progress in material prosperity and the eastern in spiritual. Many centuries after Suez has again been opened up to renew the lost connection between the east and the west to fulfil the purposes of a beneficent Providence.

As *Bháts* or eulogists in the present days sing in praise of heroes and dynasties so in the old days the Rig Veda was sung by the *Rishis* or sages and the assembled people heard with rapture the glories of their forefathers. In explanation of the discontinuance of the Vedic songs and psalms in India I can only say what I myself think on the subject. In many places of the Rig Veda mention is made of bovine food which the antagonists of the Panis were in the habit of taking. I am not sure if the word *go* at first meant cattle generally, but it is certain that subsequently it represented the *cows* only. And it is easy to conceive how the study of the Rig Veda came to be interdicted as containing obnoxious passages when cow-killing was considered a great sin—at least in the *Pauranic* age. In fact the Rig Veda fell into disuse with the introduction of the worship of the cow, nay the unfortunate householder who dared to possess the work was cursed to death from thunder and lightning. The result was that at last not *only the*, doomed Rig Veda, but the entire Vedas fell into oblivion leaving behind only an unshaken veneration for them in the minds of the people of the country.

Professor Sergi holds that the ancient civilisation of Europe is derived from the coasts of Africa and he does not accept the theory that the Aryan civilisation was the first and most ancient in the scale. I believe I have been able to show in this examination of the Rig Veda—which is a repository of facts and not fiction—that it was not from Central Asia, as is ordinarily supposed, but from India—the land of the Ilibis, the Panis, the Asuras, the Angiras and others—that the light of civilisation spread far and wide to wake up the whole world to progress and enlightenment.

THE END.

APPENDIX.

I.

The Phœnicians derived their name from Phœnicia, meaning the inhabitants of Phœnicia. The diphthong œ in the word shows that with the sound of *o* (as in *ŏrder*) it should read as Phŏnicia, and with the sound of *e* as Phēnicia. It is thus clear that by some the word was pronounced as Phŏnicia and by others as Phēnicia, and Phŏnicia had its origin in Phŏnis. The pronunciation of *P* and *Ph* are so closely allied that it is not unoften that the one takes the place of the other. *Ph* is *P* hard. The conclusion therefore is that *Pănis* is only a different form of *Phŏnis*, and the *Panis* of old were known as the Phœnicians in later days. In fact the word Phœnician has sprung from the word *Panis* which was the original name of the race. The country inhabited by the *Panis* came to be known as *Pănisé* or *Pănisiă*—transformed into Phŏnicia or Phœnicia, and as time went on the inhabitants of Phœnicia were called Phœnicians instead of *Panis*.

The word *Panic* or *Punic* is also derived from the word *Panis*. It is therefore clear that those who had been known as *Panis* in ancient India, were even after their settlement in Phœnicia, called *Punic* by the Indo-Aryans and the Romans. And this again leads to the further conclusion that the *Suktas* in the Vedas relating to the *Panis* or *Panik* were composed long before the settlement of the race in Phœnicia. The Western scholars admit that the Phœnicians traded with India, but this was many years after the composition of the Vedas and not before.

II.

Two eminent scholars of the day have already expressed their opinion on the subject of this treatise regarding the historical aspect of the Vedas. I append them below as they may encourage others like me in this interesting study.

1. Translation of a letter in Bengali addressed to the author by Mr. R. C. Dutt, C.I.E., late a member of the Indian Civil Service :—

I have read your essay on the Panic War. I am glad to see the scholarship and research you have brought to bear on the subject.

I see nothing improbable in the theory that there was race called *Păni* or *Panis*, that the Indian Aryans seized their cows, and that many of the *Suktas* of the Rig Veda were composed to record historical events. In fact your exposition seems more plausible than that of Prof. Max Muller. But I am unable to decide which of these two expositions is correct : indeed I cannot say if it is possible to come to a decision on the subject after so many thousand years.

To what nation or race did the *Panis* belong, if they were really men ? You say they were Phœnicians. A good many proofs are wanted before the statement can be accepted. That the Phœnicians always came to ancient India by the land route: that they quarrelled and fought with the Indian Aryans, and that the latter knew them as *Panis* or, that the Phœnicians have in their own works mentioned the Aryans living on the banks of the Indus—these are conclusions which require to be amply demonstrated. I do not say that your theory is a groundless one, but still it is only a theory for the present. Hundreds of hill tribes inhabited Afghanistan, and it is not improbable that they quarrelled with the Indian Aryans for cattle (cows), and that some of them were referred to as the *Panis* in the *Suktas* of the Vedas.

I cannot accept your meaning of the word Saramá

correct. It may be taken to mean the Dawn even if the word *Pani* signifies some hill tribe or a trading people— 'At dawn of day the Aryans discovered the concealed cows and recovered them with the help of Indra.'

There can however be no doubt that the word *go* means *cows* if your interpretation of the word *Pani* be correct.

Sd. ROMESH CHUNDER DUTT
May 1, 1902.

[The Phœnicians dwelt in some part of Afghanistan long before they colonised Phœnicia, and the wars described in the Vedas refer to those days. Defeated in those wars or for some other reasons they migrated westwards and founded the colony of Phœnicia. Or it may be that Phœnicia was their principal colony in those remote Vedic days, and after their defeat in the wars referred to in the sacred books they removed there for good. Mr. Dutt's suggestion, therefore, that the Phœnicians came to India by land, is not borne out by my conclusions —Author.]

2. The following appeared in the columns of the *Indian Mirror* (Calcutta), of the 22nd May 1902, from the pen of the eminent Sanscrit scholar Prof. Satis Chandra Acharya Vidyabhusan M. A. of the Presidency College (Calcutta):—

" It was nearly ten years ago that I marked with surprise several passages in the Rig Veda (as for instance, in Mandala VI, Sukta 53) where the word *Pani* repeatedly occurred. Looking into the commentary of Sayanacharya, I found the word *Pani* interpreted as *Vanij*, a merchant. In the Chapter on *Unádi* suffixes in *Panini's* Sanskrit Grammar, the word *Vanij* was found to be derived from the root *Pan*. I then suspected that the word *Pani*, meaning a merchant and occurring in the Rig Veda, might refer to the Phœnician race. Eventually I gave expression to the fact in several places, and lately in the introduction to my edition of Kachchayana's Pali Grammar. I expressed my view on the subject with great diffidence. Now I am very glad to find my view confirmed by our learned friend, Babu Rajeswar Gupta, Head Master of the Rangpore Normal School, and Editor of *Anjali*, who has published a long and interesting article on the subject in the *Chaitra* number of his journal. The article is an admirable one and is a product of deep researches into the Vedic literature. It reflects great credit on the scholarship of the writer and has brought to light some very important facts of earliest history."

OPINIONS ON THE BOOK.

* * * I shall study the charming little book together with ıy pupils with great interest.

Prof: P. Deussen,.
Kiel, Germany.
13—5—05.

I return you my best thanks for sending me your very nteresting little book on the Rigveda which I have read with great pleasure. I agree with you in the principle (historical nterpretation) but I cannot follow you in the details.

I wish you would give us more treatises of the same kind, or it has always been my opinion that India principally is for he Indians.

(Hon'ble Prof: Dr) V. Fausboll,.
Copenhagen, Denmark.
20—5—05.

Please accept my ackowledgements for your interesting ooklet on the Rigveda. * * *

(Lt. Col.) L. A. Waddell,. (L. L. D. I. M. S.)
London, England.
8—5—05.

---

* * * I have read your book with greatest interest adıiring the diligence and ingenuity with which you are dig-n. up history from the Rigveda. * * *

(Hon'ble) A. Barth,.
Paris, France.
22—5—05.

Pray accept my best thanks for your little book entitled The Rigveda a history". It is a good thing to endeavour to tract as much history as possible from so old and imortant a work as the Rigveda. * * *

A. Macdonell,. (PH. D.)
Professor of Sanskrit, Oxford University.
7—5—05.

• • • I have no opinion of my own on vedic topics, bu I always feeled strongly disinclined to adopt all the mytholo gical conclusions of MaxMuller. It is quite certain that ther is in the Rigveda a complicate mixing of historical event and legendary traditions. So far I agree with you.

Lowis de la Vallee,.
Professor at the University of Ghent.
24—5—05.

• • • No doubt a certain number of the hymns of th Rigveda are legendary or even historical; but these are very small minority. I cannot see that the presence of sucl hymns invalidates the natural view that the Rigveda as whole is a book of praise.

C. Bendall,.
Professor of Sanskrit, Cambridge.
6—5—05.

• • • My own opinion is that there is not sufficient evidence in the Rigveda to justify the very far-reaching conclu-clusions at which you arrive.

E. I. Rapson,.
British Museum, London.
13—5—05.

• • • I perused the book and found it to contain much that is original and deserving of careful attention. We ought to be all obliged to you for the production.

Sarada Charan Mitra,. (Justice)
Calcutta High Court.
13—4—05.

• • • I have read it with much pleasure. The question you raise is a highly interesting one; but your theory require further proof before it is generally accepted.

(Sir) Gooroo Das Banerjee (Kt. M. A. D. L.)
Calcutta, 30th January 1905.

• • • *The* researches of Babu Rajeswar Gupta make *quite clear that* the Panis formed a race with whom the

Indu-Aryans had a fight. It is quite legitimate to theorise about the identity of this race and though the theory in this respect of Babu Rajeswar Gupta may not be conclusive that it is worthy of every consideration does not admit of doubt.

* * *

The researches of Babu Rajeswar Gupta are quite original and they will do credit to any scholar.

Purnendu Narayan Singha (M. A. B. L.)
Bankipur, 5th June 1905.

---

* * * The Rigveda a history which I have read with interest and pleasure.

R. T. H. Griffith,. (PH. D.)
Late Principal, Benares College.
Kotagiri, 5th June 1905.

Babu Rajeswar Gupta's brief history of "The Rigveda" shows a certain amount of patient and original research. He attempts to prove that the Phœnicians had their earliest home in India and were driven out only after a fierce and bloody struggle. "The Rigveda" he says, "is therefore not a poem only but a history describing these and other wars". The Essay affords food for reflection.

The Engishman, Saturday, March 18, 1905.

The Rigveda—A History by Rajeswar Gupta.

* * *

The author has interpreted the Rigveda in a way altogether original and fruitful of useful results. To be able to dig up the valuable treasures buried in the sacred books of the East is not an easy task. The patient and successful researches of the author have entitled him to the gratitude of all antiquarians and particularly the Hindus. We recommend the book under notice to the reading public.

The Hindu Patriot, Monday March 13, 1905.

The Rigveda—A History by Rajeswar Gupta.

* * * His studies and investigations in the field are truly commendable.

The Amrita Bazar Patrika, Tuesday May 9, 1905.

The Rigveda—A History ——Our friend Babu Rajeswar Gupta's interesting pamphlet on the Rigveda as a history, indicates that, in imitation of the example of Western scholars, the study of higher criticism of our religious books has been pursued with vigour by our countryman and is making important developments. * * * The theory is a novel one and needs confirmation by the more renowned authorities on the subject. The appendix contains a letter from the pen of Mr. R. C. Dutt who seems sympathise with the writer.

The Unity & the Minister. May 7, 1905.

The Rigveda—A History by Rajeswar Gupta.

* * *

There can not be a second opinion that the subject deserves the most careful study of all oriental scholars, as if it is proved that the Rigveda s ia history then our distant forefathers can be absolved from the charge of not keeping an account of what happened among them. But we content ourselves by quoting Mr R. C. Dutt's opinion on the question and humbly reminding our friend, the author, that we expect much light from him on the old as well as the new "Veda" for the redemption of humanity.

The World and the New Dispensation, May 14, 1905.

The Rigveda—A History by Rajeswar Gupta.

* * *

We trust these statements will be fully and impartially discussed by the scholars of the East and the West, and Babu Rajeswar Gupta will devote more time and thought to substantiate them with more proofs and researches. The mastery of facts and the wise handling of them with the stamp of originality and deep thought which he has displayed in this little paper bids fair to put him into the front rank of the antiquairians and philologists, and we only hope that he will be spared to continue his noble work. [Remarks on the original essay.]

The East, April 19, 1902.